Paper Plate Bible Crafts

Paper Plate Bible Crafts

58 easy-to-do ideas for 5-7s

Anita Reith Stohs

About the author

Anita Reith Stohs is the author of children's picture books, journal articles, curricular materials and nearly 40 teaching resources and activity books. A teacher by profession, her time-tested ideas come from more than 25 years of classroom experience with primary-aged children and young people with special needs, as well as with her own children and grandchildren.

Text copyright © Anita Reith Stohs 2010
Illustrations copyright © Carolyn Braun 2010
The author asserts the moral right
to be identified as the author of this work

Published by
The Bible Reading Fellowship
15 The Chambers, Vineyard
Abingdon OX14 3FE
United Kingdom
Tel: +44 (0)1865 319700
Email: enquiries@brf.org.uk
Website: www.brf.org.uk
BRF is a Registered Charity

ISBN 978 1 84101 698 6

First published 1992 by Concordia Publishing House, 3558 S. Jefferson Avenue, St Louis MO 63118-3968, USA

UK edition first published 2010
10 9 8 7 6 5 4 3 2 1 0

Acknowledgments
Unless otherwise stated, scripture quotations are taken from the Contemporary English Version of the Bible published by HarperCollins Publishers, copyright © 1991, 1992, 1995 American Bible Society.

Scripture quotations taken from the Holy Bible, New International Version, copyright © 1973, 1978, 1984, 1995 by International Bible Society. Used by permission of Hodder & Stoughton Publishers, a member of the Hachette Livre UK Group.

A catalogue record for this book is available from the British Library

Printed in Singapore by Craft Print International Ltd

Contents

Jesus' life of love

Jesus gives new life

The Church grows

Special days

Bible index

Introduction

Children learn by doing. A craft project following a Bible story can help to reinforce the words a child has just heard and provide a visual reminder of God's continuing love and care.

The easy-to-do projects in this book, all using readily available paper plates and simple craft materials, are designed to help young children grow in the knowledge and love of God.

Any size paper plate can be used for the projects, although younger children may find it easier to work on larger plates. Unless specified, the plates should be paper, not polystyrene. Paper plates are cheap, sturdy and easy to colour with crayons or felt-tipped pens.

Read through the instructions given with each project, but feel free to make changes as you see fit. Illustrations accompanying the text are for reference only: encourage the children to make projects that are unique, not imitations of the book, the teacher, or each other. Let the infinite variety that God shows in the way he creates be our guide to releasing the children's own creativity.

God made our wonderful world

The heavens and the earth

Bible story: Genesis 1:1

Activity: A picture

You will need:

- One paper plate per child
- Coloured crayons or felt-tipped pens
- Sticky-backed stars (optional)
- Hole punch
- World atlas (for reference)

Instructions

Draw a circle around the inside of the plate's rim. Draw lines to divide the circle into continents and oceans of the world. Draw mountains, cities and familiar landmarks.

Colour in the land and the water. Around the rim of the plate write the words from Genesis 1:1: 'In the beginning God created the heavens and the earth.'

Draw in and colour a sun, moon, stars and comets on the remaining space around the plate rim. Add sticky-backed stars if you wish.

Punch a hole in the top of the paper plate. Hang the finished plate up as a reminder that God made our wonderful world.

Talk about

Talk about the wonderful world that God has made.

Other ideas

- Torn card or tissue paper could also be used to make land and water.
- Instead of Genesis 1:1, write 'He's got the whole world in his hands' around the plate.

Lights in the sky

Bible story: Genesis 1:14–18

Activity: A wall-hanging

You will need:

- Three 20cm paper plates per child
- Yellow, tan and orange wool
- Scissors
- Glue
- Ribbon (75cm length per child)
- Hole punch

Instructions

Cut four pieces of yellow wool to 20cm lengths and glue to the centre of one plate as shown. Glue an X shape first and then add one horizontal and one vertical length to form a star.

On a second plate, coil orange and/or yellow wool around the centre section of the plate. Cut orange and yellow wool into pieces the width of the plate rim. Glue the wool around the rim for the sun's rays.

On a third plate, glue coiled circles of yellow and/or tan wool to make craters on the moon. If you wish, cut out a section of the plate to make a crescent shape.

Glue all three plates down on the ribbon, about 3cm apart. Punch a hole in the top of the uppermost plate and tie a piece of wool through it to form a loop. Hang the wall-hanging up to show the lights that God placed in the sky.

Talk about

Talk about how the sun, moon and stars separate day from night and show the time of the seasons, special days and years.

Other ideas

- Instead of using wool, colour in the sun, moon and star with felt-tipped pens.
- Allow each child to choose and make just one plate picture.
- Invite the children to put their plates on a display board as part of a creation project.
- Use the plates to illustrate other Bible passages about God's creation of lights in the sky, such as Psalm 136:7–9.
- Use the star plate on its own for the star of Bethlehem.

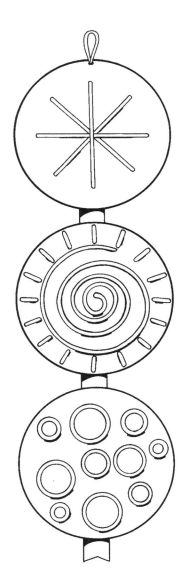

Days of creation

You will need:

- Two paper plates per child
- Coloured crayons or felt-tipped pens
- Scissors
- Ruler
- Pencil
- Magazine pictures
- Glue
- Split-pin paper fasteners
- Hole punch

Instructions

Cut off the rim of one of the paper plates. Use the ruler and the pencil to divide the circle that is left into six equal pie-shaped wedges.

Cut and glue the magazine pictures on to the sections to illustrate each day of creation. Each wedge should illustrate a single day of creation, but don't put them in any particular order.

Use a split-pin paper fastener to attach the circle with the pictures to the centre of the other plate. On the rim of the outside plate, draw an arrow pointing in towards the centre. Take turns to ask someone else what God made on a specific day of creation. The person answering the question then turns the arrow to the right picture.

Talk about

Talk about the different things that God made on each of the days of creation.

Other ideas

- For a creation plaque, use only one paper plate. Draw a circle of pictures illustrating the sequential days of creation in the centre of the plate and write the number of the day on the rim above each picture.
- Invite the children to draw in their own pictures for each day of creation.

See what God made

Bible story: Genesis 1:11–12 and 20–25

Activity: A nature mobile

You will need:

- One plastic or polystyrene plate per child
- Ballpoint pen
- Coloured crayons or felt-tipped pens
- Objects from nature, such as feathers, pine cones, bark, dried flowers or seashells
- Scissors
- Wool
- Sticky tape
- Hole punch

Instructions

Use a pen to punch a hole through the middle of the paper plate, then make holes around the rim with a hole punch.

Write 'See what God made' around the rim of the plate. Choose some natural objects to hang around the plate to make a mobile. Cut a piece of wool for each of the objects, using a variety of lengths. Tie one end of each piece of wool to an object and tie the other end through a hole in the paper plate.

Hold the plate so that the writing is on the top. Cut one more piece of wool and thread it through the hole in the middle of the plate. Knot the wool on the underside of the plate and secure with sticky tape.

Hang the mobile up to show the wonderful world God made for us to touch and see.

Talk about

Talk about the wonderful things that God has made for us to enjoy in nature.

Other ideas

- Instead of a mobile, make a wind-chime with objects that make a noise when blown on or hit together.
- Invite the children to draw their own pictures of things that God has made and hang them from the plate.

God makes the flowers grow

Bible story: Genesis 1:11

Activity: A sunflower collage

You will need:

- One paper plate per child
- Yellow wool
- Scissors
- Glue
- Green and brown card
- Sunflower seeds
- Pencil
- Hole punch

Instructions

Cut lengths of yellow wool to fit the rim of the plate and glue in place as shown. Cut a circle of brown card to fit inside the rim and glue in place. Cover the brown card with sunflower seeds and glue in place. Explain to the children that God makes the big sunflower grow from a tiny seed.

Using the shape in the illustration as a guide, cut a stem and leaves out of the green card and glue them to the bottom of the plate. Write the words 'God makes the flowers grow' across the leaves and stem as shown. Punch a hole in the top of the plate and hang it up.

Explain to the children that the sunflower turns towards the sun as the sun moves across the sky. The sunflower is a reminder to look constantly to God as we go through the day.

Talk about

Talk about things we can do to help us keep our eyes upon God.

Other ideas

- Cut petals out of yellow card.
- Use yellow plates and glue the sunflower seeds to the centre.
- Use different coloured beans and paper to make other kinds of flowers.

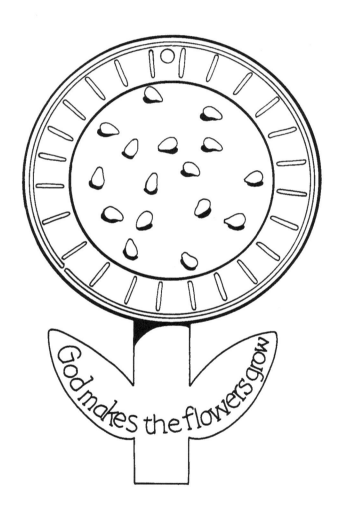

At home in God's creation

You will need:

- One paper plate per child
- Coloured crayons or felt-tipped pens
- Brown and white card
- Scissors
- Glue
- Pencils

Instructions

Cut the paper plate in half. (The children can use the pieces to make one or both of the animals.) Draw a spiral on one half of the plate for the snail's shell and draw rounded squares on the other half to make a tortoise shell.

To make a tortoise, draw a head, a tail and two legs on brown card. Cut them out and glue them on to the tortoise shell as shown. To make a snail, draw a head with two antennae and a large snail foot on white card. Cut them out and glue them on to the snail shell. Draw eyes and a smile on each head.

Talk about

Talk about God's good plans for giving hard shells to provide homes for the snail and the tortoise. Talk about how God helps other animals to provide homes for themselves.

Other ideas

- Use wool to cover the snail and tortoise shells.
- Make the shapes on the tortoise shell out of pieces of card.
- Use a whole paper plate to make a tortoise by cutting out and gluing a head, four legs and a tail on to the front of the plate. Turn the plate upside down and colour a shell pattern on to the back.

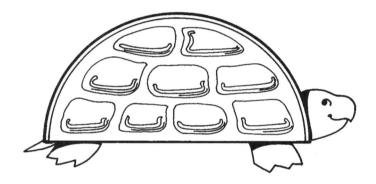

God's helpful creatures

You will need:

- One paper plate per child
- Black, white and red coloured crayons or felt-tipped pens
- Black and white card
- Scissors
- Glue
- Ballpoint pen
- Wool

Other ideas

- Use black wool for the legs and antennae.
- Cut spots out of black card to glue on to the ladybird.

Instructions

Invite the children to decide which creature they want to make.

To make the ladybird, colour a red background and black spots on to the back of a paper plate. Cut a head out of black card and colour in two white eyes. Cut six short black strips of card for legs. Fold each strip down once to make a knee and up once for a foot. Cut two thin strips of card for antennae. Glue the head, legs and antennae on to the paper plate.

To make the spider, colour the back of a paper plate black. Cut eight long black strips of card and fold them accordion-wise as shown. Glue the legs in place as shown. Cut two white ovals for eyes and draw a black spot on each one. Fold the ovals down on one end and glue them on to the back of the plate as shown.

Use a pen to punch a hole in the middle of the ladybird and spider models. Thread a loop of wool through the hole and hang up the creepy-crawly creature.

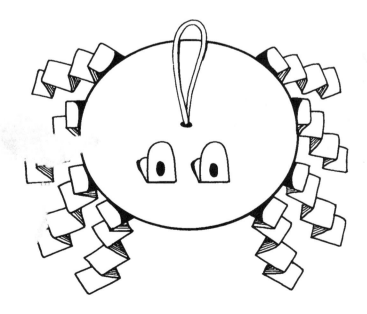

Talk about

Talk about how God made ladybirds and spiders along with all the other creatures.

Under the sea

Bible story: Genesis 1:20

Activity: Octopus and jellyfish models

You will need:

- One half of a paper plate per child
- Coloured crayons or felt-tipped pens
- Scissors
- Crêpe paper in an assortment of light colours, including grey and white
- Glue
- Hole punch
- Wool

Instructions

With the straight edge facing downward, draw eyes and a smile on to the plate half.

For the jellyfish, cut light-coloured tentacles out of crêpe paper and glue them on to the straight edge of the plate half. For the octopus, cut eight grey or white legs out of crêpe paper and glue them on to the straight edge of the plate half.

Punch a hole at the top of the plate half and thread a piece of wool through it. Knot the wool to form a loop and hang up the sea creature.

Talk about

Talk about other wonderful creatures that God put into the sea.

Other ideas

- Look at pictures of other ocean animals and make more paper plate creatures.
- Put the models on to a display board with the title 'God's sea creatures'.

God made me!

Bible story: Genesis 1:26–31

Activity: A stick puppet

You will need:

- One 20cm paper plate per child
- Coloured crayons or felt-tipped pens
- Pencils
- Scissors
- Glue
- Wool in assorted colours, including yellow, brown, orange and black
- Craft sticks

Instructions

Ask the children to use a pencil to draw their own eyes, nose and mouth on to a plate, then colour the features and the background of the plate to represent themselves.

Invite the children to choose some wool, the same colour as their own hair. Cut the wool into lengths to represent their own hairstyle and glue in place. (Pigtails can be made by punching a hole on each side of the plate, pulling several strands of wool through each hole and tying them in place.)

Glue the craft stick to the back of the plate and use a felt-tipped pen to write 'God made me special' on the stick.

Talk about

Talk about how each one of us is unique and very special in God's eyes.

Other ideas

- Use felt-tipped pens rather than pencils to draw in the features.
- Add scraps of fabric, ribbon or card to give more detail.
- A darning needle could be used by older children to add the wool for hair.
- Make Bible characters in the same way and use them to act out Bible stories.

God cares for his people

A rainbow in the sky

Bible story: Genesis 9:12–17

Activity: A rainbow plaque

You will need:

- One paper plate per child
- Brown card
- Blue, brown and assorted balls of wool in rainbow colours
- Scissors
- Glue
- Hole punch

Instructions

Using the illustration as a guide, draw and cut out an ark from a piece of brown card. Cut a piece of brown wool and glue it in a curve across the middle of the plate to make a mountain top. Glue the ark above the piece of wool.

Glue several pieces of blue wool in wavy lines below the mountain top for water. Cut pieces of wool in rainbow colours. Glue them in a curve above the ark to form a rainbow.

Punch a hole at the top of the plate. Thread a piece of wool through the hole and make a loop to hang up the rainbow plaque. Encourage the children to use their plaques as a reminder that God cared for Noah and he also cares for us.

Talk about

Talk about ways in which we can know God's care for us.

Other ideas

- Use wax crayons to colour in the rainbow and ark. Then brush over them with a blue watercolour wash, made by diluting paint with water.
- Use coloured tissue paper to make the water and the rainbow.
- Colour in the rainbow and water with felt-tipped pens before adding the wool.

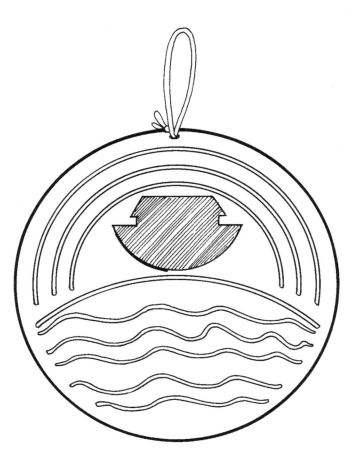

Moses is born

You will need:

- One paper plate per child
- Coloured crayons or felt-tipped pens
- Rulers
- Scissors
- Sponges
- Small dishes
- Orange or brown poster paint
- Rubber printing stamps
- Scraps of fabric
- Glue
- Blue wool

Instructions

Fold the paper plate in half. To make the top of the basket, draw a line 3cm below the folded edge of the plate.

Using the illustration as a guide, draw an outline of baby Moses above the line, making sure that a part of the head and body touch the fold. Cut out the head and body as illustrated and draw in Moses' face.

Place the sponge in the dish and pour a small amount of orange or brown paint on to the sponge. Use the rubber stamp to print a basket-weave pattern on the lower half of the plate. Allow to dry.

Cut scraps of fabric and glue them in place to make Moses' blanket. For the water, cut pieces of blue wool and glue them just above the curved part of the basket.

Rock the basket backwards and forwards and pretend that baby Moses is rocking in the river, waiting for Pharaoh's daughter to come and find him.

Talk about

Talk about the way God took care of baby Moses and the ways in which he also takes care of us today.

Other ideas

- Colour the basket with crayons or felt-tipped pens.
- Tear brown paper into small pieces and glue them over the plate to make the basket pattern.
- Use food colouring to dye macaroni pieces yellow and blue. Allow to dry and then glue on to the plate to make the basket and the water.
- Glue vertical pieces of green wool on to the plate to make bulrushes.

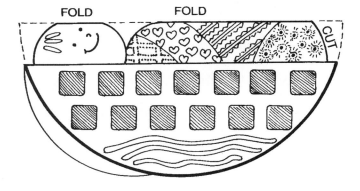

God speaks to Moses

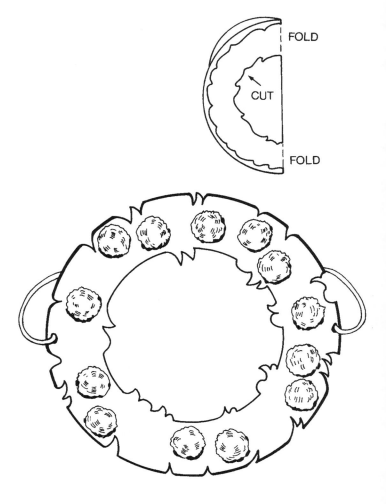

Bible story: Exodus 3:1–12

Activity: A Moses mask

You will need:

- One paper plate per child
- Pencils
- Scissors
- Shirring elastic
- Cottonwool balls
- Glue
- Hole punch

Instructions

Fold the paper plate in half. Use a pencil to outline Moses' hair and beard on one side of the plate. Cut out the face and hair, keeping the paper plate folded as shown. Unfold the plate and punch holes in each side with the hole punch.

Cut a piece of elastic to fit the child's head. Tie the ends of the elastic to each side of the mask. Glue cottonwool balls on to the mask for a beard and hair.

Invite the children to wear their masks while you tell the story of how God asked Moses to help him lead the people out of Egypt.

Talk about

Talk about ways in which God speaks to us today.

Other ideas

- Adapt the mask for other Bible characters and use it to tell their stories.
- Colour in the hair and beard with felt-tipped pens or crayons.
- Use string or wool instead of elastic to secure the mask around the child's head.

Miriam's song

Bible story: Exodus 15:19–21

Activity: Miriam's tambourine

You will need:

- Two paper plates per child
- Coloured crayons or felt-tipped pens
- Wool
- Sticky tape
- Hole punch
- Dried beans

Instructions

Decorate the outside of both plates with felt-tipped pens or crayons. Write 'Sing to the Lord' on the outside of one of the plates and draw wavy lines, for the waters of the Red Sea, on the outside of both plates.

Hold the plates together and punch holes about 2.5cm apart around the edges. Cut a piece of wool about 60cm in length. Tie a knot at one end and tape the other end to act as a needle. Lace the wool through the holes around the edge of the plates.

Before knotting the wool in the final hole, slip several dried beans inside the tambourine. Use the tambourine to sing a song of praise to God.

Talk about

Talk about ways in which we can praise God.

Other ideas

- Illustrate the outside of the plates with a picture of the Israelites passing through the Red Sea.
- Print words from a favourite song of praise on the tambourine.
- Add several streamers made from crêpe paper to decorate the tambourine.
- Staple or glue the plates together.
- Put small jingle bells inside the tambourine for a Christmas rhythm instrument.

Food from heaven

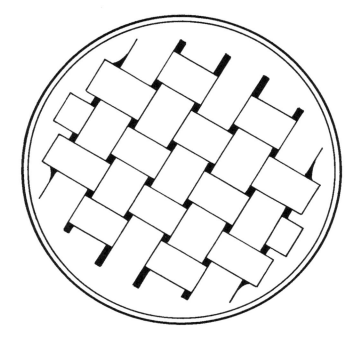

You will need:

- One paper plate per child
- Scissors
- Coloured card
- Small marshmallows

Instructions

Cut parallel lines 2.5cm apart across the inner circle of the plate. Cut strips of card in one colour or a variety of colours.

Weave a strip of card across the cut lines on the plate. Trim the ends of the strip and glue it down. Weave a second strip across the cut lines, next to the first, in an alternating pattern. Continue until the plate is filled.

Put small marshmallows on to the plate and eat them, pretending they are manna.

Talk about

Talk about ways in which God provides for our daily needs.

Other ideas

- Vary the colours and sizes of the paper strips for a more interesting design.
- Alternate the paper strips with ribbon.
- Glue down white pieces of paper or polystyrene packing pieces to make the manna.

David plays for King Saul

Bible story: 1 Samuel 16:14–23

Activity: David's harp

You will need:

- One paper plate per child
- Coloured crayons or felt-tipped pens
- Scissors
- Rulers
- Wool
- Pencils
- Sticky tape
- Hole punch

Instructions

Fold the plate in half and draw a pattern to make half the harp, as shown. Keeping the plate folded, cut out the harp outline. Unfold the plate and write 'Praise God' on the harp. Decorate the harp with musical notes.

Use a ruler to draw equal parallel marks, 1.25–2.5cm apart, at the top and bottom of the harp's opening. Use the hole punch to make holes over the marks.

Cut a long piece of wool, tie a knot in one end and tape the other end to act as a needle. Thread the wool through a hole at the top of the harp. Pull the wool down to the hole below, go through it and come up through the hole beside it. Go back up to the top and continue until the last harp string is in place. Knot or tape the string on the back of the harp.

Invite the children to pretend to play their harps as you sing songs of praise to God together.

Talk about

Talk about songs of praise that the children know, and sing them together.

Other ideas

- Cut out the outside of the harp and then draw in the centre and strings.
- Use a darning needle to punch the holes and thread the wool.

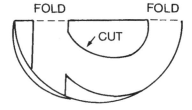

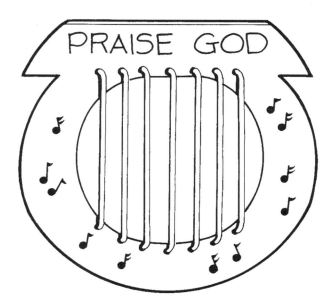

David and Jonathan

You will need:

- Paper plates (one between two children)
- Coloured crayons or felt-tipped pens
- Scraps of fabric
- Scissors
- Stapler
- Glue
- Drinking straws

Instructions

Cut the plate in half to make two puppets. For each puppet, bend the half-plate round and staple the flat sides together to make a cone. Draw a line to separate the head from the body. Cut out scraps of fabric and glue them on to the body part of the cone to make a robe. Draw in a face and the hair.

Use scissors to make arm holes in each puppet. Put a drinking straw through the arm holes and trim it to the right length for the arms. Use two puppets to act out the story of David and Jonathan.

Talk about

Talk about friends.

Other ideas

- Make an additional puppet for King Saul.
- Omit the scraps of fabric, and colour in the robes instead.
- Glue a drinking straw or a craft stick to the inside of each puppet to make stick puppets.

The Lord is my shepherd

Bible story: Psalm 23

Activity: Little lamb model

You will need:

- One paper plate per child
- Black felt-tipped pens
- Scissors
- White and black card
- Cottonwool balls
- Glue
- Paperclips
- Sticky tape

Instructions

Draw an oval shape on white card and cut it out. Use a felt-tipped pen to draw on an eye and mouth. Glue the oval on to the paper plate for a head. Cut an ear and four feet out of black card and glue them to the plate as shown.

Glue cottonwool balls over the plate for the lamb's woollen coat. Tape a paperclip to the back of the lamb so that it can be hung on a wall. Explain to the children that the lamb can remind us that Jesus, our good shepherd, watches over us all the time.

Talk about

Talk about the ways in which a shepherd cares for his sheep and ways in which Jesus cares for us.

Other ideas

- Instead of cottonwool, coil or swirl pieces of white wool over the lamb.
- Make a flock of sheep for a display board and add the words 'We are Jesus' little lambs'.
- Use the model in connection with the story of David the shepherd boy or Jesus' stories about sheep and shepherds.

Food from a raven

Bible story: 1 Kings 17:1–6

Activity: Stick puppets

You will need:

- One paper plate per child
- Coloured crayons or felt-tipped pens
- Scissors
- Glue
- Yellow card
- Black wool
- Drinking straws or craft sticks
- Sticky tape

Instructions

Cut the paper plate in half. Use the felt-tipped pens or crayons to draw in a raven's eyes on one half of the plate. Cut a square out of yellow card, fold it in half and glue it on to the raven to make a beak. Cut small pieces of black wool and glue them on to the raven for feathers.

Draw Elijah's face on the second half of the plate. Cut longer pieces of black wool and glue them on the straight edge to make Elijah's beard. Place a drinking straw or a craft stick at the back of each puppet and tape it in place. Use the puppets to act out the story of the ravens bringing bread and meat to Elijah.

Talk about

Talk about unexpected ways in which God provides for us.

Other ideas

- Use black card instead of wool to make the raven's feathers and Elijah's beard.
- Colour the feathers and beard with felt-tipped pens or crayons.

- Use half-plate puppet designs to illustrate other stories from the Bible.

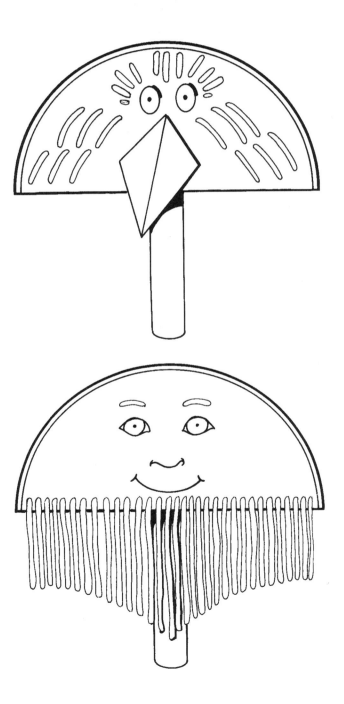

God sends the rain

Bible story: 1 Kings 18:1–46

Activity: A rain cloud collage

You will need:

- One paper plate per child
- Coloured crayons or felt-tipped pens
- Scissors
- Glue
- Blue wool
- Sticky tape
- Cottonwool balls
- Hole punch

Instructions

Cut the paper plate in half. Write 'God gives us rain' around the back rim of one half of the plate.

Cut the wool into pieces measuring 10–15cm in length. Glue the lengths of wool along the straight edge of the same half of the plate to make rain, and then tape the wool in place to secure it firmly.

Glue the remaining plate half to the back of the first half. Glue cotton wool balls over the front plate. Punch a hole in the top of the collage and tie a piece of wool through the hole to form a loop. Hang up the clouds as a reminder that rain is a gift from God.

Talk about

Talk about rain and the good things that it brings.

Other ideas

- Use tinsel instead of wool to make the rain.
- Use just one plate half, with or without the writing on it.
- Using a display board, pile several plate halves together to create a thunderstorm mural, or make a long rain cloud by overlapping a row of plates.

Queen Esther saves her people

Bible story: Esther 1—3

Activity: A stick puppet

You will need:

- One paper plate per child
- Felt-tipped pens
- Scissors
- Glue
- Stapler
- Yellow and black card
- Pencils
- Tin foil
- Drinking straws or craft sticks
- Sticky tape

Instructions

Cut a line to the centre of the paper plate. Turn the plate to the back and overlap the cut sides slightly to make a cone. Staple the sides together. Use felt-tipped pens to draw in eyes, a nose and a mouth on the outside of the cone.

Cut strips of black card and wrap them around a pencil to curl them. Glue the strips on to the paper plate for hair. Cut out a yellow crown and glue it on top of the puppet. Tear small pieces of foil and glue them over the crown.

Secure a straw or craft stick to the back of the puppet with sticky tape. Use the puppet to have Queen Esther tell the story of how God used her to save her people.

Talk about

Talk about the ways in which God uses us to do good things.

Other ideas

- Use wool for the hair.
- Glue pieces of coloured card on to the crown.
- Scrunch up small pieces of coloured tissue paper and glue them on to the crown.
- Make holes at the top and bottom of the puppet and stick a drinking straw through the holes.
- Make stick puppets to illustrate other Bible characters and animals.

Ezekiel's wheel

Bible story: Ezekiel 1:4–28

Activity: Circular loom weaving

You will need:

- One paper plate per child
- Scissors
- Rulers
- Pencils
- Hole punch
- Wool in bright colours
- Sticky tape

Instructions

Cut off the rim of the paper plate. Use a ruler to mark off an odd number of spaces, 1.5–2.5cm apart, around the rim. Use a hole punch to punch holes in the marked spaces.

Cut a long length of wool and tie a knot in one end. Tape the other end to use as a needle. Pull the wool through a hole and bring it over to the opposite hole. Come up through the next hole and go across to the opposite hole. Repeat until all the holes are connected. Bring the last thread to the centre and tie it around the crossing threads. Let the loose thread hang at the back.

Starting at the centre, weave over and under the crossing threads. Leave the loose ends at the back when you change threads. When finished, weave the loose threads into the back of the weaving. Cut the weaving off the paper plate and, if desired, tie a fringe to each loop around the outside of the weaving.

Talk about

Talk about how God gave Ezekiel a message to tell others. Encourage the children to use their wheels as a reminder to share with others the good news of Jesus' redeeming love.

Other ideas

- Leave the weaving on the paper plate and write 'Ezekiel saw the wheel' around it.
- Use yellow and orange yarn to make a sun, to tell the story of creation.
- Use circular weaving as a symbol of God's eternal love.

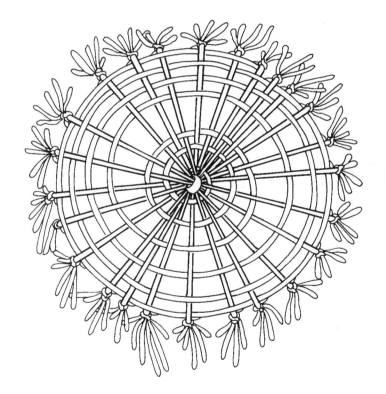

Daniel and the lions

Bible story: Daniel 6:1–28

Activity: Paper plate masks

You will need:

- Two paper plates per child
- Coloured crayons or felt-tipped pens
- Scissors
- Orange and brown card
- Glue
- Hole punch
- Wool

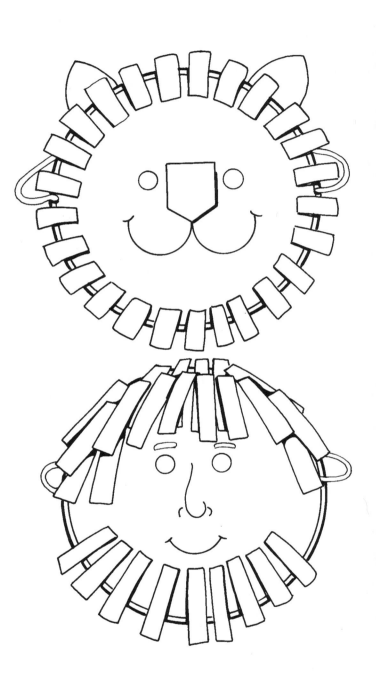

Instructions

Cut eyeholes in both paper plates. Cut two brown ears and a nose for the lion, as shown, and glue the pieces on to one of the plates. Use a felt-tipped pen or crayon to draw in the lion's mouth. Cut orange strips and glue them around the rim of the plate to make a mane.

On the other plate, use a felt-tipped pen or crayon to draw in eyes, a nose and a smile for Daniel. Cut strips of brown paper and glue them on for hair and a beard.

Punch holes on each side of the two masks and tie a piece of wool measuring 20–25cm in length to each hole. Tie on the masks to act out the story of Daniel in the lions' den.

Talk about

Talk about how we can stay faithful to God in difficult times.

Other ideas

- Use wool instead of card to make the lion's mane and Daniel's hair.
- Make an additional mask for King Darius.
- Use paper plate masks to act out other Bible stories.
- Hang up the mask as a wall plaque.

Jesus is born

Getting ready for Jesus

Bible story: Luke 1:5–25

Activity: An Advent wreath

You will need:

- One paper plate per child
- Scissors
- Green tissue paper
- Glue
- Pencils with integrated rubbers
- Purple, pink and yellow card

Instructions

Cut the centre from the paper plate, leaving the rim intact. Cut squares of green tissue paper and glue them on to the rim of the plate. Older children can twist them around a pencil rubber and glue them to the plate. Younger children can simply crumple the tissue into balls or glue on flat squares.

Cut three purple rectangles and one pink rectangle out of card for the candles. Cut 0.5cm tabs at the bottom of each candle, bend up the tabs and glue the candles to the wreath. Cut out four yellow flames. Glue a flame on to a candle at the beginning of each week in Advent.

Talk about

Talk about what we do to get ready for Jesus at Christmas.

Other ideas

- Use a green paper plate to make the wreath.
- To hang up the wreath, leave out the candles and add balls of red tissue paper for berries. Glue on a bow made out of wool or ribbon.
- Use torn pieces of green card to cover the wreath. Add shell pasta shapes dipped into red food colouring for berries.

An angel appears to Mary

Bible story: Luke 1:26–38

Activity: An angel ornament or handprint puppet

You will need:

- Half a paper plate per child
- Coloured crayons or felt-tipped pens
- Scissors
- Stapler
- Pencils
- Paper doilies
- Glue
- White craft foam
- Glitter

Instructions

Staple the edges of the half plate to make a cone shape. Draw a line to separate the robe and head. Draw a face and hair.

Trim a paper doily to fit the angel's body and glue in place. Trace and cut out two craft foam hand prints. Swirl glue on to each hand print and sprinkle on glitter. Glue the hand prints to the back of the angel for wings.

Stand the angel as a table decoration, place it on top of a Christmas tree, or hang it as an ornament.

Talk about

Talk about the good news that the angel brought to Mary.

Other ideas

- Colour the angel with crayons or felt-tipped pens.
- Use glitter or sequins to decorate the angel's robe. Add wool, lametta or tinsel for hair.
- Glue pieces of the paper doily over the wings.
- Completely cover the hand prints with glue and then dip them into glitter.
- Use the angel to tell additional Bible stories in which angels appear.

Happy birthday, Jesus

Bible story: Luke 2:1–7

Activity: A wool-wrapped wreath

You will need:

- One paper plate per child
- Plastic lids
- Coloured crayons or felt-tipped pens
- Scissors
- Glue
- Hole punch
- Green and red wool

Instructions

Cut out the centre of the plate, leaving only the rim. Using a plastic lid as a guide, draw a smaller circle on the centre of the plate and cut it out. On the small circle write 'Happy birthday, Jesus'. Punch a hole at the top of the small circle and tie on a piece of wool.

Tie a long piece of green wool around the rim of the plate and wrap the long end of the wool around and around the rim. Repeat until the rim is covered, finishing with a knot to secure.

Glue small coils of red wool to the wreath for berries. Make a bow out of wool and glue it to the bottom of the wreath.

Punch a hole in the lower edge at the top of the wreath and use a piece of wool to hang the small circle from the hole. Attach a loop of wool to the top of the wreath and hang up the wreath to celebrate Jesus' birthday.

Talk about

Talk about ways in which we celebrate birthdays.

Other ideas

- Make the wreath out of a green paper plate.
- Use glitter, wool and sequins to make the wreath.
- Cut the centre out of a plastic lid and wrap the outer circle of the lid with wool to make a small tree ornament.

Celebration party hat

Bible story: Luke 2:1–7

Activity: A party hat

You will need:

- One paper plate per child
- Coloured crayons or felt-tipped pens
- Scissors
- Stapler
- Coloured stickers
- Wool
- Hole punch

Instructions

Cut a pie-shaped wedge out of the plate. Overlap the cut edges to make a cone-shaped party hat. Size the hat to fit the child who will wear it, but don't staple the hat at this stage.

Lay the hat flat and decorate it with stickers and coloured felt-tipped pens or crayons. Write 'Happy birthday, Jesus' or other appropriate words on to the hat. Cut several short pieces of wool, knot them together at one end and staple them at the top of the hat.

Overlap the cut edges again to make a hat and staple the edges together. Punch holes in the bottom of two sides of the hat. Tie a piece of wool, 20–25 cm in length, into each hole. Wear the hat to a Christmas party.

Talk about

Talk about things we need for a party.

Other ideas

- Decorate the hat with torn pieces of card instead of stickers.
- Cover the hat with Christmas biscuit cutter outlines.

Jesus is born

Bible story: Luke 1:26—2:20

Activity: Paper plate lacing

You will need:

- One paper or polystyrene plate per child
- Coloured crayons or felt-tipped pens
- Ballpoint pens
- Wool
- Sticky tape
- Paperclips

Instructions

Use the felt-tipped pens or crayons to draw and colour a picture from the Christmas story on to the plate. Poke holes with the end of a pen along the outline of the picture. Make the holes close together around curves and further apart on straight sections.

Cut a piece of wool approximately 60cm in length. Knot one end and tape the other to serve as a needle. Lace the design. Tape a paperclip to the back of the plate and display the picture on a wall.

Talk about

Talk about the different parts of the Christmas story.

Other ideas

- Let each child illustrate a different part of the Christmas story. Line up the finished plates in the correct sequence.
- Cut out a picture from a Christmas card and glue it to the plate. Then punch holes around the picture for lacing.
- Use paper plate lacing to illustrate other Bible stories.

A gift for Jesus

Bible story: Matthew 2:1–12

Activity: Bag puppet

You will need:

- Two paper plates per child
- Paper bags
- Coloured crayons or felt-tipped pens
- Scissors
- Glue
- Scraps of fabric
- Gold chain, incense or perfume bottle (optional)

Instructions

Keeping the opening at the top, draw a face on a paper bag. Glue the bag on to one plate as shown, so that the plate forms a turban.

Cut the second plate in half. Glue one half at the bottom of the face to serve as the top of a robe. Use fabric scraps to cover the turban and the robe.

Let the wise man puppet tell of his search for baby Jesus. Put the gold chain, incense or perfume inside the bag. Pull it out as the wise man tells how he gave his gift.

Talk about

Talk about what gifts of love we can give to Jesus.

Other ideas

- Colour the paper plate with felt-tipped pens or crayons.
- Cut the robe out of paper and glue it to the bottom of the face.
- Make more wise men and act out the story. (The Bible doesn't tell us how many wise men there were: make as many as your imagination or resources allow.)

We have seen his star

Bible story: Matthew 2:1–12

Activity: A sewing project

You will need:

- One paper or polystyrene plate per child
- Rulers
- Pencils
- Yellow wool
- Scissors
- Darning needles

Instructions

Use a ruler and pencil to mark off 2.5cm intervals around the inside rim of the paper plate. Thread a needle with a piece of wool measuring approximately 60cm in length. Knot one end of the wool.

With the knot at the back, push the needle through one of the pencil marks. Pull the wool through and then push the needle down through the mark at the opposite side of the plate. Repeat the process, pushing the needle up through the next mark and back across the plate to the opposite hole. Continue until all the holes are filled. Tie a loop of wool to the plate to hang up the star.

Talk about

Talk about how we can use the stars for navigation.

Other ideas

- Use a pen to punch a circle of holes around a polystyrene plate. Tape the end of a piece of wool to serve as a needle.
- Vary the length and colour of the wool for a more interesting effect.
- Use with other Bible stories involving stars, such as God's promise of descendants to Abraham (Genesis 15:1–6).

Jesus' life of love

Jesus' baptism

Bible story: Matthew 3:13–17

Activity: A dove mobile

You will need:

- One paper plate per child
- Pencils
- Scissors
- Glue
- Hole punch
- Polystyrene packing pieces
- Wool

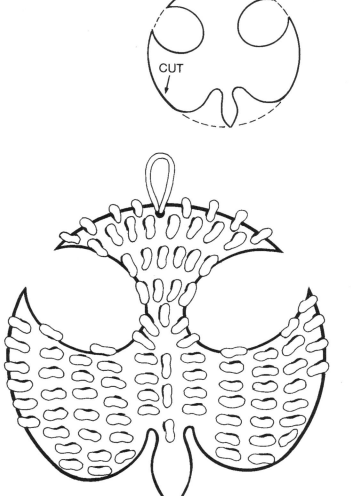

Instructions

Using the illustration as a guide, use a pencil to draw a dove shape on the paper plate. Cut it out. Glue polystyrene packing pieces over both sides of the dove.

Punch a hole in the dove's tail and tie a piece of wool through the hole to hang up the mobile.

Talk about

Talk about baptism and what it means.

Other ideas

- Use the dove for other stories in which a dove appears, such as Noah's ark (Genesis 8:8–11).
- If they have been baptised, invite the children to write the date of their baptism on the dove shape and hang the dove up as a reminder of that day.
- Cover the dove with white wool or crumpled pieces of white tissue paper.

Fishing for people

You will need:

- One paper plate per child
- Coloured crayons or felt-tipped pens
- Scissors
- Glue
- Hole punch
- Card
- Wool

Instructions

Use either a half or a whole paper plate to make the fish. Use a felt-tipped pen or crayon to draw in the eyes and scales. Write the words 'Come with me!' on the sides of the fish.

Cut out card fins and a card tail. Glue the fins and tail on to the fish.

Punch a hole in the top of the fish and tie a piece of wool through the hole. Hang up the fish as a reminder to tell others about Jesus.

Talk about

Talk about ways in which we can tell others about Jesus.

Other ideas

- Cut coloured tissue paper to make the scales. Glue them to the fins and tail by brushing each piece with a mixture of water and white glue.
- Use fringes of paper or wool to make the fish's tail and fins.
- Draw in the eyes and scales with a light-coloured crayon and then go over them with a darker water-colour wash, using watercolour paint or diluted poster paint.

- Use the fish to tell other Bible stories about fish or fishing, or as part of a creation mural.

Jesus' helpers

Bible story: Luke 6:12–16

Activity: Jesus' helpers masks

You will need:

- Half a paper plate per child
- Coloured crayons or felt-tipped pens
- Scissors
- Wool
- Hole punch
- Elastic

Instructions

Choose a disciple for the mask to represent. Cut eye holes in the mask, positioned as shown. Use felt-tipped pens or crayons to draw a nose and a mouth. Punch holes in each side of the mask.

Size the elastic to the child who will wear the mask. Tie the elastic to the holes on each side of the mask.

Let the children wear their masks as you tell the story of how that particular disciple was a helper for Jesus.

Talk about

Talk about ways in which we can be Jesus' helpers today.

Other ideas

- Use two pieces of wool or string to tie on the mask.
- Omit the eye holes and glue the paper plate to a stick or straw to use as a puppet.
- Use card to make the hair.
- Adapt the mask to represent other Bible characters or animals.

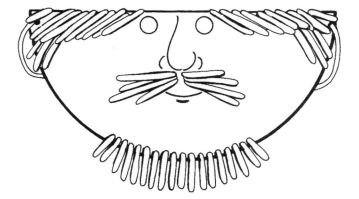

Take time to pray

Bible story: Matthew 6:9–15

Activity: A prayer clock

You will need:

- One paper plate per child
- Coloured crayons or felt-tipped pens
- Scissors
- Card
- Split-pin paper fasteners

Instructions

Write numbers for the clock hours around the rim of the paper plate. Ask the child to trace his or her hand (fingers together) on to a piece of card. Cut out the outline and write on the hand shape, 'Take time to pray'.

Use a split-pin paper fastener to attach the hand to the centre of the plate. Move the hand around the clock face.

Talk about

Talk about prayers that can be said at different times of the day.

Other ideas

- Use the prayer clocks when praying with the children or teaching about prayer.
- Write Bible verses about prayer on the hand.

Look at the birds in the sky!

Bible story: Matthew 6:25–27

Activity: A paper plate bird

You will need:

- One paper plate per child
- Coloured crayons or felt-tipped pens
- Scissors
- Glue
- Card in assorted colours
- Pencils
- Craft feathers

Instructions

Draw a circle on a piece of card to make the bird's head. Cut it out. Use a felt-tipped pen or crayon to draw eyes. Glue the circle to the top centre of the paper plate.

Fold a small piece of card in half and cut a triangle, with the base of the triangle on the fold to make a double beak. Glue the bottom part of the beak on to the bird, leaving the top part to pop up. Cut feet for the bird and glue them to the bottom of the plate.

Write 'God cares for me' on the centre of the paper plate. Glue craft feathers on each side of the bird. Colour in the rest of the bird if desired.

Talk about

Talk about ways in which God cares for us.

Other ideas

- Instead of using feathers, make wings by fringing card or crêpe paper. Some birds, such as penguins or owls, may look better with thicker, paper wings.
- Make different varieties of birds for a creation mural.

Look how the wild flowers grow

Bible story: Matthew 6:28–34

Activity: A paper plate flower

You will need:

- One paper plate per child
- Pieces of sponge
- Water
- Tissue paper in assorted colours
- Green card
- Coloured crayons or felt-tipped pens
- Scissors
- Glue

Instructions

Dab water on the paper plate with a piece of sponge. Cut or tear pieces of coloured tissue paper and place them on the wet plate. Allow to dry and then pull the tissue paper off (the plate will retain the colour from the tissue paper).

Leave the plate whole or cut it in half. Cut the rim of the plate to form petals, according to the type of flower chosen (see examples as shown).

Cut a stem and leaves out of green card. Glue the stem and leaves to the base of the flower. Write 'God cares for me' on the leaves and the stem.

Talk about

Talk about the difference between things we need and things we want.

Other ideas

- Use coloured paper plates to make the flowers.
- Glue coloured pieces of torn card over the plates instead of using wet tissue paper.
- Glue seeds or beans in the centres of the flowers or to outline the petals.
- Make a flower creation mural.

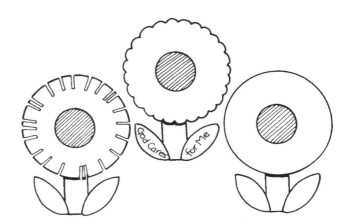

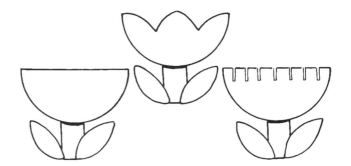

From a little seed

Bible story: Mark 4:30–32

Activity: A mosaic plate

You will need:

- One paper plate per child
- Coloured crayons or felt-tipped pens
- Dried split peas
- Glue
- Hole punch
- Wool

Instructions

Write 'The mustard seed' around the bottom rim of the plate. Draw birds around the rest of the rim. In the top centre of the plate, draw a circle to represent a tree top. Draw a horizontal line to represent the ground across the bottom third of the plate. Draw a vertical line from the circle to the ground to serve as a tree trunk.

Glue a single split pea at the bottom of the vertical line. Glue dried split peas inside the circle to fill in the tree. Punch a hole at the top of the plate and tie a piece of wool through the hole.

Hang the mosaic plate as a reminder of how God's kingdom grows like a big plant from a tiny seed.

Talk about

Talk about ways that God's kingdom has grown through the years and still is growing today.

Other ideas

- Glue a real mustard seed at the base of the tree trunk.
- Outline the tree top, trunk and ground with wool.
- Cut little pieces of craft feathers and glue them to the drawings of birds.
- Omit the split peas and fill the tree with green wool, torn pieces of card or wadded pieces of tissue paper.
- Colour the picture with crayons or felt-tipped pens.
- Use brown beans to outline the tree trunk.

Seeds on good ground

You will need:

- One paper plate per child
- Coloured crayons or felt-tipped pens
- Scissors
- Glue
- Blue card
- Dried spaghetti
- Round pasta shapes

Instructions

Cut a circle out of blue card to fit the inside of the paper plate. Glue it in place. Write 'The seed on good ground' around the rim of the plate.

Break the spaghetti into pieces and glue on to the middle of the plate for grain stems. Glue round pasta shapes around the top of the spaghetti for heads of grain.

Glue pasta around the rim of the place for decoration. Display the plate as a reminder of how we grow in love when we listen to God's word.

Talk about

Talk about the parable and its meaning.

Other ideas

- Use other kinds of pasta or round cereal to make the grain heads.
- Colour the pasta with food colouring, let it dry and then glue on to the plate.

The prodigal's pig

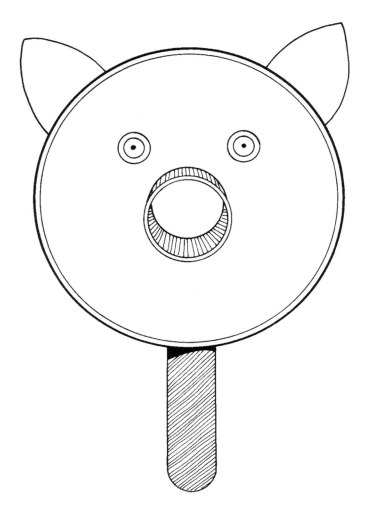

Bible story: Luke 15:11–32

Activity: A stick puppet

You will need:

- One 20cm paper plate per child
- Pink card
- Pink felt-tipped pens, crayons or poster paint
- Scissors
- Glue
- Craft sticks
- Sticky tape (optional)

Instructions

Cut a strip of card 5cm wide by 12cm long. Roll the strip round and glue the edges to make a ring of card. Cut three 1.5cm slits on one side of the ring. Fold the flaps in and glue the ring to the middle of the paper plate.

Colour the middle of the inside of the ring pink using a pink felt-tipped pen, crayon or poster paint. Cut ears out of pink card and glue them to the top of the paper plate, positioned as shown.

Cut out and glue two circles for eyes. Glue or tape a craft stick to the back of the plate. Hold the pig puppet and have him tell the story of the prodigal son.

Talk about

Talk about forgiveness—what it means to forgive and what it means to be forgiven.

Other ideas

- Use a pink plate to make the puppet.
- Draw in the eyes.
- Tear up pieces of pink tissue paper and glue them on to the plate with a mixture of white glue and water.
- Use a larger plate, with a paper cup for the pig's snout.

Get ready for Jesus

Bible story: Matthew 25:1–13

Activity: A lamp

You will need:

- Half a paper plate per child
- Coloured crayons or felt-tipped pens
- Scissors
- Glue or sticky tape
- Pencils
- Red cellophane

Instructions

Cut a hole out of one side of the half paper plate, as shown, to make a handle. Write 'I am ready' on to the lamp. Decorate the lamp as desired.

Cut flame shapes from red cellophane and crinkle them. Tape or glue the flame shapes on to the top of the lamp.

Display the lamp as a reminder that our faith in Jesus makes us ready for him to come again.

Talk about

Talk about what we can do to be prepared for Jesus.

Other ideas

- Cut a red flame out of red card.
- Cover a cardboard flame with tin foil and glue it on to the lamp.
- Draw and colour the lamp on a whole paper plate.
- Use a coloured paper plate for the lamp.
- Omit the handle and make a temple lamp to use with the story of Samuel (1 Samuel 3:1–18).
- Write 'Let your light shine' on the lamp. Tell of ways we can show God's love to others.
- Use the lamp to illustrate the songs 'This little light of mine' and 'Give me oil in my lamp'.

Lord of wind and waves

Bible story: Matthew 8:23–27

Activity: A boat

You will need:

- Half a paper plate per child
- Coloured crayons or felt-tipped pens
- Scissors
- Piece of white paper
- Drinking straws
- Sticky tape

Instructions

With the straight side of the plate half at the top, draw high waves across the bottom of the plate.

Cut a square sail out of white paper. Write, 'Jesus is Lord of the wind and waves' on the sail.

Tape a drinking straw to the back of the plate and tape the sail to the straw above the plate.

Talk about

Talk about keeping safe and use the boat as a reminder as you tell the story of Jesus keeping his friends safe in the storm.

Other ideas

- Add a second straw to make a cross at the top of the sail.
- Use blue wool to make the waves.
- Draw a cross on the sail instead of writing the words.
- Use a tan-coloured paper plate to make the boat shape.
- Use clothes pegs for people and act out other Bible stories involving boats.

Praise God for pizza

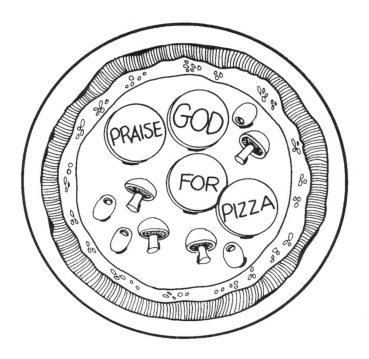

Bible story: John 6:5–15

Activity: A pizza plate

You will need:

- One paper plate per child
- Coloured crayons or felt-tipped pens, including grey
- Scissors
- Glue
- Brown, red and yellow card

Instructions

Colour the rim of the plate grey for the pan. Cut a brown card circle to fit inside the rim for the crust. Cut a smaller red card circle for tomato sauce. Cut a still smaller wavy yellow card circle for cheese. Add shapes and colours as desired for other pizza toppings. Glue in successive order the crust, tomato sauce, cheese and toppings.

Use a felt-tipped pen or crayon to write, 'Praise God for pizza' on the topping shapes.

Talk about

Talk about favourite foods.

Other ideas

- Dye macaroni pieces yellow with food colouring and glue on to the pizza for cheese.
- Use with other stories that illustrate our thankfulness for God's gift of food, such as Exodus 16:1–36 (the story of the manna) or 1 Kings 17:1–6 (Elijah and the ravens).

Let down the nets

Bible story: Luke 5:1–11

Activity: A crayon-resist plaque

You will need:

- One paper plate per child
- Coloured crayons
- Blue watercolour paint or poster paint
- Paintbrushes
- Hole punch
- Small pieces of wool

Instructions

Use light-coloured crayons to draw fish on the inside of the plate. Write the words 'Let down the nets' around the rim of the plate. Draw a grid over the fish for a net.

Make a watercolour wash by diluting blue watercolour paint or poster paint with water. Brush over the entire plate.

Punch a hole in the top of the plate and tie a piece of wool through it. Hang the picture up as a reminder of how Jesus chooses us to be his friends and helps us to catch people for God.

Talk about

Talk about being a friend of Jesus.

Other ideas

- Instead of drawing a net, fit fruit netting over the plate after the paint has dried.
- Cover the plate with clingfilm and use as a creation picture of the fish that God made.
- Use the picture to tell of another time when Jesus filled the nets with fish (John 21:1–14).

Jesus loves me

Bible story: Mark 10:13–16

Activity: A framed picture

You will need:

- One paper plate per child
- Coloured crayons or felt-tipped pens
- Scissors
- Plastic lids or saucers (the size of the centre of the paper plate)
- Pictures of Jesus
- Pencils
- Clear self-adhesive plastic
- Hole punch

Instructions

Place the lid or saucer over the picture of Jesus and use a pencil to trace around it. Cut out the picture.

Trace and cut out a second circle from self-adhesive plastic. Cover the picture with the self-adhesive plastic.

Write 'Jesus loves me' around the bottom of the plate. Decorate the rest of the rim with hearts and crosses.

Punch a hole in the top of the plate and hang up the picture as a reminder of Jesus' love.

Talk about

Talk about how we know that Jesus loves us.

Other ideas

- Let the children draw their own picture of Jesus.
- Sing 'Jesus loves me' when the plate is finished.
- Omit the self-adhesive plastic.
- Use wool or rickrack to decorate the rim of the plate.
- Use paper plates to frame other pictures of Bible stories.

Jesus comes to see Zacchaeus

Bible story: Luke 19:1–10

Activity: A tree picture

You will need:

- One paper plate per child
- Green tissue paper
- Scissors
- Pencils
- Glue
- Brown card
- Craft foam
- Two clothes pegs per child
- Coloured crayons or felt-tipped pens

Instructions

Cut tissue squares, twist them around the end of a pencil and glue them to the plate. Cut a rectangular tree trunk from brown card and glue it to the bottom of the plate.

Cut two pieces of craft foam the size of a clothes peg. Use crayons or felt-tipped pens to draw Jesus on one piece of craft foam and Zacchaeus on the other. Glue each piece of craft foam on to a clothes peg.

Use the clothes pegs and tree to tell the story of Jesus and Zacchaeus.

Talk about

Talk about how meeting Jesus can change our lives.

Other ideas

- Omit the craft foam and use felt-tipped pens and fabric scraps to make Jesus and Zacchaeus out of the clothes pegs.
- Cover the tree with torn pieces of green card.
- Make a pipe-cleaner snake and then use two clothes pegs for Adam and Eve to tell the story of people's first disobedience (Genesis 3:1–24).

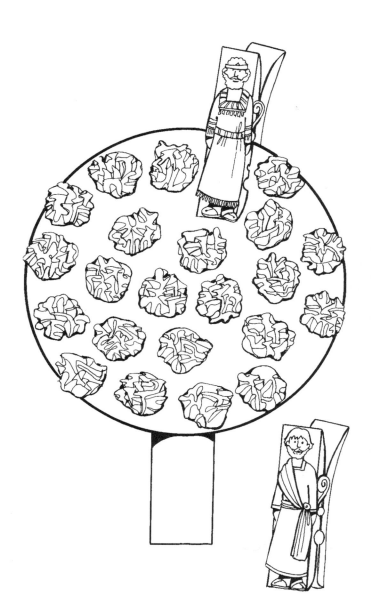

Jesus gives new life

The Lord's supper

Bible story: Matthew 26:26–30;
Luke 22:19–20

Activity: A Communion cup

You will need:

- One paper plate per child
- Coloured crayons or felt-tipped pens
- Scissors
- Glue
- Yellow watercolour paint or poster paint
- Water
- Paintbrushes

Instructions

Cut the paper plate in half. Cut one of the halves in half again. Cut a circle out of one of the quarter-sized pieces. Draw a cross in the middle of it. Glue the circle at the top of the plate half as shown. Glue the second quarter piece as shown to make a base for the cup.

Write the words 'Poured out for you' on to the cup. Decorate the rim and base of the cup as desired.

Dilute the paint with water and brush a watercolour wash over the cup.

Talk about

Talk about how your church celebrates the Lord's supper.

Other ideas

- Use only crayons or felt-tipped pens to decorate the cup.
- Use a coloured paper plate to make the cup.

Good Friday

Bible story: Luke 23:32–43

Activity: A mosaic

You will need:

- One paper plate per child
- Coloured crayons or felt-tipped pens
- Scissors
- Glue
- Green, brown and red card

Instructions

Cut halfway around the inside rim of the paper plate. Tear up pieces of green card and cover the inside centre of the plate. Write 'He died for all' along the bottom rim of the plate. Fold up the half circle so that it stands out from the plate.

Cut brown card into strips. Use the strips to make three crosses. Tear red card into pieces and glue them on to one of the crosses.

Glue the three crosses to the top half of the circle, placing the cross with the red card in the centre. Glue some more pieces of green card at the bottom of the crosses as shown.

Talk about

Talk about the events of Good Friday.

Other ideas

- Instead of tearing the pieces of card, cut them into squares.
- Glue pieces of coloured tissue paper or ribbon on to the picture.
- Omit the card and colour the picture with crayons or felt-tipped pens.
- To make a one-dimensional plaque, draw the hill and crosses on to the plate and fill in with squares of coloured card.

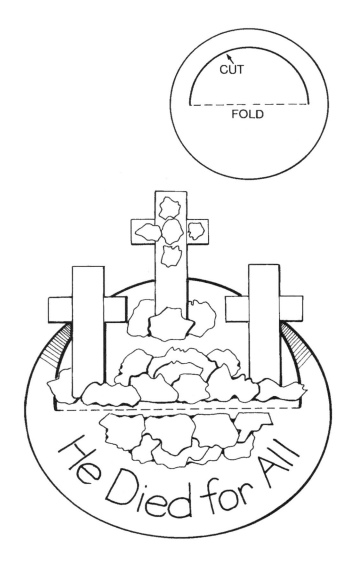

Jesus died for me

You will need:

- One paper plate per child
- Scissors
- Rulers
- Pencils
- Variegated purple wool
- Darning needles

Talk about

Talk about why Jesus died for us.

Other ideas

- Use bright colours for a victorious Easter cross.
- Cut 1.5cm deep slits into the sides of the plate and start the cross from there. Tape the end of the weaving yarn to serve as a needle.

Instructions

Use a pencil and ruler to mark off 1.5cm spaces along a 5–6cm width at the top of the inside rim of the paper plate. Measure off the same number of spaces along the bottom of the inside rim. Do the same on the left and right sides of the plate.

Cut a piece of wool 60cm in length, knot one end and thread the other end through the needle. Bring the needle up through one of the marked spaces at the top of the plate, with the knot on the back, and go across to the marked space opposite it. Bring the needle through that mark and come up through the next mark. Continue until all the vertical marks have been sewn.

Do the same with the marks for the horizontal part of the cross, weaving over and under the vertical threads of wool already in place. Alternate the weaving each time you change direction. Continue until all the horizontal threads are in place.

Starting at one end of the cross, weave a piece of wool over and under the threads until you get to the other side. Turn around and weave back, going over and under the opposite way from the line of wool you have just woven. Continue until the whole cross has been covered with wool.

When the weaving is completed, loop a piece of wool through the top of the plate and hang up the cross as a reminder that Jesus died for us.

Jesus rose for me

Bible story: Matthew 28:1–10

Activity: An Easter basket

You will need:

- One paper plate per child
- Coloured crayons or felt-tipped pens
- Scissors
- Glue
- Hole punch
- Wool
- Sticky tape
- Coloured card in an assortment of colours
- Craft sticks

Other ideas

- Make flowers out of tissue paper and glue on to the craft sticks.
- Draw and decorate paper Easter eggs to glue on to the sticks.
- Change the wording on the basket to use as a gift for Mothering Sunday.

Instructions

Cut off the outer rim of the paper plate. Cut the inner circle in half. On the outside of one half plate, write 'Jesus is alive'. Use crayons or felt-tipped pens to add flowers around the words.

Draw flowers on the outside of the other half plate. Hold the plates together and punch holes 2.5cm apart around the round edges.

Cut pieces of wool 50cm in length. Knot one end of the wool and tape the other to serve as a needle. Lace the wool around the plates.

Cut paper flowers out of card and glue them to the craft sticks. Put the card flowers in the Easter basket.

Talk about

Talk about spring flowers and other signs of new life at Easter time.

Easter joy

You will need:

- One paper plate per child
- Coloured crayons or felt-tipped pens
- Scissors
- Pencils
- Sticky-backed plastic
- Coloured tissue paper
- Hole punch
- Wool in assorted colours

Instructions

Use a pencil to draw a butterfly in the centre of a paper plate. Cut it out so that a butterfly-shaped space is left in the plate. Trace the butterfly pattern on to a piece of sticky-backed plastic. Expand the drawing by 1cm. Repeat these steps on a second piece of plastic.

Take the backing off one piece of plastic and fit the plastic over the butterfly shape cut into the paper plate. Tear or cut pieces of tissue paper and stick them on to the sticky-backed plastic. Cover the front of the butterfly shape with the second piece of plastic.

Use felt-tipped pens to write 'Easter joy' or a Bible verse from the Easter story around the rim of the plate. Punch a hole in the top of the plate. Loop a piece of wool through it and hang up the butterfly.

Talk about

Talk about the butterfly as a symbol of Jesus' resurrection.

Other ideas

- Add pieces of wool to the butterfly.
- Use coloured card or ribbon instead of tissue paper.

He is risen

Bible story: Luke 24:1–8

Activity: An empty egg

You will need:

- Two paper plates per child
- Coloured crayons and felt-tipped pens
- Pieces of sponge
- Watercolour paints
- Water
- Scissors
- Split-pin paper fasteners

Instructions

Use light-coloured crayons to decorate the outside of one plate to look like an Easter egg. Use a piece of sponge to paint a watercolour wash (paint diluted with water) over the plate.

Cut the first plate in half. Fasten the sides to the bottom centre of the second plate with a split-pin paper fastener as shown.

Open up the egg and write 'He is risen' on the bottom plate.

Talk about

Talk about the message of the angel on that first Easter morning.

Other ideas

- If desired, decorate the outside of the bottom plate too.
- Use stickers or felt-tipped pens to decorate the egg.
- Wet the plate with water and then put coloured pieces of tissue paper over it. Remove the tissue when dry.
- Glue on pieces of coloured tissue paper with a mixture of water and PVA glue.

Jesus is alive

Bible story: John 20:1–18

Activity: A balloon plate

You will need:

- One paper plate per child
- Coloured crayons or felt-tipped pens
- Scissors
- PVA glue
- Water
- Tissue paper in an assortment of colours
- Paintbrushes
- Clingfilm
- Wool

Instructions

Cut squares of tissue paper in an assortment of colours.

Dilute the glue with water. Lay one square of tissue paper on the plate at a time. Paint the glue wash over one square at a time until the plate is covered.

When the glue is dry, use a felt-tipped pen to write 'Jesus is alive' on the plate.

Wrap clingfilm around the plate. Tape a piece of wool to the bottom of the plate.

Talk about

Talk about the good news that Jesus is alive.

Other ideas

- Decorate two plates and staple them together to form a two-sided balloon.
- Decorate the balloon with crayons, felt-tipped pens, paints or pieces of coloured card.
- Make the balloon with a coloured paper plate.
- Write the words 'Jesus is taken to heaven' to tell the ascension story.

Jesus is taken into heaven

Bible story: Acts 1:1–11

Activity: A spiral

You will need:

- One paper plate per child
- Coloured crayons or felt-tipped pens
- Pencils
- Scissors
- Wool
- Hole punch

Instructions

Use a pencil to make a dot in the centre of the plate. Beginning at the dot, draw a spiral line, filling the plate.

Use felt-tipped pens or crayons to write the words 'Jesus went up into heaven' along the spiral. Decorate the spiral with felt-tipped pens or crayons.

Cut out the spiral. Punch a hole at the top, loop in a piece of wool and hang up the spiral.

Talk about

Talk about the story of Jesus' ascension.

Other ideas

- Glue pieces of cottonwool on to the spiral to make clouds.
- Cover the spiral with torn pieces of coloured card.
- Use a spiral to celebrate other Christian holidays, such as Christmas, Easter or Pentecost. Write an appropriate Bible verse on the spiral and then decorate it.

The Church grows

Tell everyone!

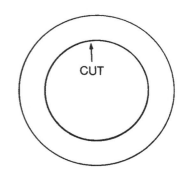

Bible story: Matthew 28:16–20

Activity: A good news frisbee

You will need:

- One paper plate per child
- Coloured crayons or felt-tipped pens
- Scissors

Instructions

Cut the rim off the plate, being careful to leave the rim intact. Write 'Jesus loves you' around the rim and decorate it.

Talk about

Throw the frisbees back and forth to each other and talk about how much Jesus loves each one of us.

Other ideas

- Use the whole paper plate to make a frisbee.
- Write Bible verses you would like to share on the frisbee.

Go to everyone in the world

Bible story: Matthew 28:16–20;
Mark 16:15–16

Activity: An op-art cross

You will need:

- One paper plate per child
- Coloured crayons or felt-tipped pens
- Mathematical compasses
- Pencils
- Rulers
- Wool
- Hole punch

Other ideas

- Use blue or green for the background colours.
- Experiment with variations in the size of the rays and circles.
- Use another Christian symbol in the centre of the plate.
- Use the same colours for the whole plate.

Instructions

Mark the centre of the plate. Outline a cross in the centre of the plate as shown. Use a pair of compasses to draw concentric circles around the plate, stopping at the rim. Use a ruler to draw rays from the centre of the plate to the rim.

Colour in alternate spaces of the cross. Colour in alternate spaces of the background using different colours from those used in the cross.

Write the words 'Into all the world' around the rim of the plate. Use a hole punch to make a hole at the top of the plate. Tie a piece of wool through the hole and hang up the cross.

Talk about

Talk about ways to take the good news about Jesus to everyone in the world.

Paul and the snake

Bible story: Acts 28:1–10

Activity: A snake puppet

You will need:

- One paper plate per child
- Coloured crayons or felt-tipped pens
- Scissors
- Glue
- Card
- Old socks

Instructions

Fold the plate in half. Cut eyes and fangs from card. Glue the eyes to the top of the plate and glue the fangs to the inside of the plate (see illustration). Draw nose holes as shown and colour in scales as desired.

Cut a strip of card the width of the plate and glue it to the back. Cut a thumb hole in the toe of an old sock and also below the fold of the plate (the child's thumb will serve as the snake's tongue). Pull the sock over the child's hand and slip his or her thumb through the thumb hole. Slide the child's hand (inside the sock) under the strip of card at the back of the puppet.

Show the child how to put his or her thumb through the hole on the inside of the plate and wiggle it for the snake's tongue. To move the puppet, the fingers need to be placed over the fold and pressure applied to open and shut the folded plate.

Talk about

Make the puppets talk to tell the story of what happened to Paul when he was shipwrecked on Malta.

Other ideas

- Use a mitten or glove instead of an old sock.
- Use the snake to tell the story of Adam and Eve (Genesis 3:1–24).
- Use pieces of felt instead of card to make the snake's features.

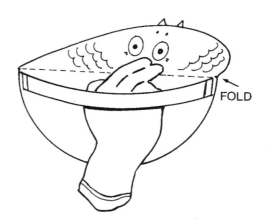

FOLD

Special days

The Trinity

Bible story: Mark 1:9–11; Matthew 28:19

Activity: A three-in-one plaque

You will need:

- Three paper plates per child
- Coloured crayons or felt-tipped pens
- Scissors
- Glue

Instructions

Cut the rims off all three plates, leaving the rims intact. Cut a slit through the rims of two of the plates. Slip the two slit plate rims around the third circle and each other to make three intertwining circles. Glue the plate rims in place.

Use felt-tipped pens or crayons to write 'Father' on one plate, 'Son' on the second plate and 'Holy Spirit' on the third plate.

Talk about

Talk about how God is three persons in one God. Use examples such as the story of Jesus' baptism (Mark 1: 9–11) or Jesus' 'great commission' in Matthew 28:19 to show how we know about the Trinity.

Other ideas

- Use three differently coloured plates.
- Decorate the rim of each plate with a symbol unique to the person of the Trinity—for example, a hand for the Father, a cross for the Son and a dove for the Holy Spirit.

Pentecost

You will need:

- One paper plate per child
- Coloured crayons or felt-tipped pens
- Drinking straws
- Poster paint in shades of red, orange and yellow
- Paintbrushes
- Wool
- Hole punch

Instructions

Pour some poster paint on to the middle of the plate. Use a straw to blow the paint into a flame design. Add additional colours as desired.

When the paint has dried, write the words 'God gives his Holy Spirit' around the rim of the plate. Punch a hole in the top of the plate and hang it up.

Talk about

Talk about what happened on the day the Holy Spirit arrived—the birthday of the Church.

Other ideas

- Sprinkle glitter over the paint or use a glitter stick.
- Draw dove shapes around the rim of the plate.

Give thanks

Bible story: Psalm 106:1 (NIV)

Activity: A grace placemat

You will need:

- One small paper plate per child
- Sheets of A4 card
- Coloured crayons or felt-tipped pens
- Scissors
- Glue
- Paper napkins
- Card in assorted colours
- Paper cups
- Sticky tape

Instructions

Glue the plate to the centre of the A4 card. Fold the napkin and glue it to the left of the plate as shown in the illustration. Cut a fork, knife and spoon out of card and glue in place as shown. Cut the cup in half and tape it to the top right-hand side of the plate. Cut out shapes of food from coloured card and glue them to the plate.

Write the words 'Give thanks to the Lord, for he is good; his love endures forever' at the top of the card.

Talk about

Talk about the good things that God gives us and favourite foods. Use Psalm 106:1 as a prayer before meal times.

Other ideas

- Be creative in cutting out food: strips of yellow paper can be folded to make chips, brown paper can be stuffed for a bun, mashed potato can be made from cottonwool and spaghetti from wool.
- Glue plastic cutlery on to the placemat and use magazine pictures of food for the plate.
- Use the plate with Bible stories about God's provision.

Give thanks to the Lord, for he is good; his love endures forever.
PSALM 106:1

Bible index

The Encyclopedia of Bible Crafts

187 fun-filled, easy-to-do craft activities for children

Edited by Laurie Castañeda

Children love doing craft activities—and children's leaders love crafts that connect children to Bible truths! This bumper collection of creative, fun-filled and easy-to-do Bible crafts is designed to inspire and enthuse leaders and children alike as they explore the Bible together.

Each tried-and-tested craft is designed to fit into any Bible-based children's work programme, whether that's on a Sunday, midweek, or a one-off special event. Every single book of the Bible is covered, with crafts to illustrate many key Bible passages. The crafts are easy to prepare, easy to do and require very little equipment or materials.

Alongside the craft activities you will also find:

- An age guide for each craft
- A Bible reference
- A Bible point
- 'You will need' list
- Handy hints
- Step-by-step instructions
- Teaching point

Includes photocopy permission for all craft templates.

ISBN 978 1 84101 590 3   £12.99
Available from your local Christian bookshop or, in case of difficulty, direct from BRF using the order form on page 79. Also visit www.brfonline.org.uk.

Also from BRF/Barnabas

Instant Games for Children

101 fun-filled children's games using just 14 everyday items

Susan L. Lingo

Play 101 new 'use-them-anywhere' games—it's as easy as 1... 2... 3.

1. Collect 14 inexpensive, everyday items such as two ping-pong balls, a bag of balloons and two skipping ropes—things that are readily available.
2. Drop the items into a bag...
3. And you're ready!

You'll always be prepared with a fun activity, child-pleasing party idea or action-packed game. They're in the bag—ready at a moment's notice!

Use the games to:

• Help children to get to know each other better
• Build friendships among classmates
• Let children burn off extra energy
• Encourage cooperation and teamwork
• Create a fun, welcoming atmosphere

All the games come complete with instructions, rules, and quick and easy explanations, so you will have your children laughing and playing in no time at all.

ISBN 978 1 84101 591 0   £6.99
Available from your local Christian bookshop or, in case of difficulty, direct from BRF using the order form on page 79. Also visit www.brfonline.org.uk.

ORDERFORM

REF	TITLE	PRICE	QTY	TOTAL
590 3	Encyclopedia of Bible Crafts	£12.99		
591 0	Instant Games for Children	£6.99		

POSTAGE AND PACKING CHARGES				
Order value	UK	Europe	Surface	Air Mail
£7.00 & under	£1.25	£3.00	£3.50	£5.50
£7.10–£30.00	£2.25	£5.50	£6.50	£10.00
Over £30.00	FREE	prices on request		

Postage and packing	
Donation	
TOTAL	

Name _____ Account Number _____

Address _____

_____ Postcode _____

Telephone Number_____

Email _____

Payment by: ❏ Cheque ❏ Mastercard ❏ Visa ❏ Postal Order ❏ Maestro

Card no ☐☐☐☐ ☐☐☐☐ ☐☐☐☐ ☐☐☐☐ ☐☐☐

Valid from ☐☐☐☐ Expires ☐☐☐☐ Issue no. ☐☐☐

Security code* ☐☐☐ *Last 3 digits on the reverse of the card.
ESSENTIAL IN ORDER TO PROCESS YOUR ORDER

Shaded boxes for Maestro use only

Signature _____ Date _____

All orders must be accompanied by the appropriate payment.

Please send your completed order form to:
BRF, 15 The Chambers, Vineyard, Abingdon OX14 3FE
Tel. 01865 319700 / Fax. 01865 319701 Email: enquiries@brf.org.uk

❏ Please send me further information about BRF publications.

Available from your local Christian bookshop.   BRF is a Registered Charity

About
brf:

BRF is a registered charity and also a limited company, and has been in existence since 1922. Through all that we do—producing resources, providing training, working face-to-face with adults and children, and via the web—we work to resource individuals and church communities in their Christian discipleship through the Bible, prayer and worship.

Our Barnabas children's team works with primary schools and churches to help children under 11, and the adults who work with them, to explore Christianity creatively and to bring the Bible alive.

To find out more about BRF and its core activities and ministries, visit:

www.brf.org.uk
www.barnabasinschools.org.uk
www.barnabasinchurches.org.uk
www.messychurch.org.uk
www.foundations21.org.uk

If you have any questions about BRF and our work, please email us at

enquiries@brf.org.uk